# Life in a Residential City

**Hélène Boudreau**

Crabtree Publishing Company

www.crabtreebooks.com

Author: Hélène Boudreau
Editor-in-Chief: Lionel Bender
Editors: Simon Adams and Molly Aloian
Proofreader: Adrianna Morganelli
Project coordinator: Kathy Middleton
Photo research: Ben White
Designer and makeup: Ben White
Production coordinator: Amy Salter
Production: Kim Richardson
Prepress technician: Amy Salter
Consultant: Amy Caldera, M.Sc., Elementary School
Publishing Consultant, Writer, and Former Teacher

Main cover photo: Residents enjoy cycling on
the recreation trail along Toronto's waterfront.
Inset cover photo: Friends in the neighborhood
often live next door.

This book was produced for Crabtree Publishing
Company by Bender Richardson White.

Photographs and reproductions:
© Getty Images: pages 17 (Alan Marsh), 18 (Alan Marsh),
20 (Alan Marsh), 24, 25 (Ron Watts), 26 (Klaus Lang),
27 (Jean Heguy)
© iStockphoto.com: cover inset-children (Nicole S. Young),
Headline image (Sangfoto), pages 1 (Gary Blakeley),
4 and 9 (Tony Tremblay), 12 (Gary Blakeley), 13 (Jon
Tarrant), 28 (Narvikk)
© www.shutterstock.com: cover inset-houses (Ruslan S.),
cover main image (Elena Elisseeva), pages 5 (Samuel
Acosta), 6 (Mark Parrott), 7 (Wade H. Massie),
8 (Natalia Bratslavsky), 10 (Helen & Vlad Filatov),
11 (Aertman), 19 (Elena Elisseeva), 22 (Aron Brand),
23 (Petr Albrektsen), 29 (Lana)
© Topfoto: pages 14 (Granger), 15 (Caro/Ruffler),
16 (Caro), 21 (Caro/Ruffler)

Acknowledgments:
The author wishes to thank the City of Toronto
authorities (www.toronto.ca) for providing
information about the city.

---

**Library and Archives Canada Cataloguing in Publication**

Boudreau, Hélène, 1969-
     Life in a residential city / Hélène Boudreau.

(Learn about urban life)
Includes index.
ISBN 978-0-7787-7393-1 (bound).--ISBN 978-0-7787-7403-7 (pbk.)

     1. City and town life--Juvenile literature.  2. Housing--
Juvenile literature.  3. Toronto (Ont.)--Juvenile literature.  I. Title.
II. Series: Learn about urban life

HT152.B69 2010          j307.3'36          C2009-906250-X

5515

**Library of Congress Cataloging-in-Publication Data**

Boudreau, Hélène.
  Life in a residential city / Hélène Boudreau.
     p. cm. -- (Learn about urban life)
  Includes index.
  ISBN 978-0-7787-7403-7 (pbk. : alk. paper) --
ISBN 978-0-7787-7393-1 (reinforced library binding : alk. paper)
1. City and town life--Juvenile literature. 2. City and town life--
Ontario--Toronto--Juvenile literature. 3. Housing--Juvenile
literature. 4. Toronto (Ont.)--Juvenile literature. I. Title. II. Series.

HT152.B68 2010
307.3'36--dc22

2009042423

---

**Crabtree Publishing Company**
www.crabtreebooks.com     1-800-387-7650

Printed in the USA/122009/BG20091103

**Published in Canada**
Crabtree Publishing
616 Welland Ave.
St. Catharines, Ontario
L2M 5V6

**Published in the United States**
Crabtree Publishing
PMB 59051
350 Fifth Avenue, 59th Floor
New York, New York 10118

**Published in the United Kingdom**
Crabtree Publishing
Maritime House
Basin Road North, Hove
BN41 1WR

**Published in Australia**
Crabtree Publishing
386 Mt. Alexander Rd.
Ascot Vale (Melbourne)
VIC 3032

# Contents

# Urban Areas

Large **towns** and **cities** are known as **urban** places. Many people live in them and they have a lot of buildings, traffic, and houses. Urban places are often divided into **zones** or special areas. Downtown zones have tall buildings and busy streets. **Residential** zones have houses and apartments where people live. Other city zones have places where people work.

▼ Cities like Los Angeles in the United States and Quebec City in Canada are busy urban **communities**. This photo shows the government buildings and waterfront of Quebec City.

Small towns and **villages** are **rural** places. They are built close to the countryside and have fewer roads and buildings. Less people, or **residents**, live there. Today, all over the world, people are moving from rural areas to the cities to work and study. This book looks at Toronto in Canada. It is a residential city—one with lots of housing zones and places to live.

# Everyday Needs

Residents form a community where they live, work, and play in a similar area. Wherever people live, they need the same basic things. They need food, shelter, and clean water to survive. They need **energy** to cook food, heat water and buildings, and run automobiles. These essential items are known as **resources.**

▼ Hong Kong has busy shopping areas. Residents can buy anything they need here, like food, electronics, and everyday items.

Urban communities need these resources for many residents. They must be supplied to every part of the city. **Natural resources** like food, energy, and building products are brought in from rural communities. Hi-tech resources like computers or communication services may be supplied from within the city or from other urban places. Rural communities need all these resources, too, but for fewer residents.

▼ City water-treatment plants never stop working. Plant workers work in set time periods day and night, to provide clean water for city residents.

The number of people living in an area is known as its **population**. Some big cities have a population of five million or more. Many people move to cities to find work, better homes, or to be close to relatives and friends. As the population grows, so does the need for new homes, houses, schools, roads, and **transportation**.

△ A city's location is very important. Being close to highways, waterways, and airports makes transporting people and shipping goods much easier.

Construction is a daily sight in urban communities. Roads and buildings are built or rebuilt as cities grow.

With more people, there is more traffic, more garbage, and more waste water from homes and offices. Cities have to find ways to deal with these issues. If they do not, there can be problems such as pollution and overcrowding, or problems with dirt and disease.

# Districts and Zones

Dividing cities into zones helps keep them organized and easier to look after. Each zone has rules about the size and use of its buildings. The **downtown** zone is the busiest part of the city. It has many offices, shopping areas, and restaurants. Residential zones have **neighborhoods**. These are smaller communities within a city that include homes, grocery stores, schools, and parks.

▼ Seen from the air, the residential part of this city is full of low-rise houses with gardens and pools.

**Factories** and **warehouses** are found in **industrial** zones. They are located away from where people live. This helps manage noise and pollution. Stores and services are grouped together in **commercial**, or business, zones. This way, shoppers can find products and services easier.

Many residents live in **suburban** zones, outside the city center, because it is cheaper or quieter. They travel to the center of the city to work.

▲ Museums, like the Louvre Museum in Paris, France, are often found in the city center. Many residents and tourists visit these sites.

# Welcome to Toronto

Toronto, Ontario, is Canada's largest city. Its 2.5 million residents come from a wide variety of cultures. They have many different traditions, customs, and beliefs. This makes Toronto one of the most **multicultural** cities in the world. The city center is home to a number of national sports teams, **company** headquarters, and theaters, as well as many stores and restaurants.

▼ The CN Tower is Toronto's best-known landmark. It stands 1,825 feet (556 m) tall, making it one of the world's tallest buildings. The tower has a revolving restaurant at the top.

▲ Toronto lies in eastern Canada on the shores of Lake Ontario. This large lake is connected to the Atlantic Ocean by the St. Lawrence River.

Toronto stretches for many miles along the coast of Lake Ontario. Its streets are laid out in a grid—a simple pattern of roads traveling from east to west or north to south. This makes traveling around the city easier. Toronto has an international airport and many major highways, which makes it a popular place for business, shipping, and travel.

▲ New businesses are established in Toronto as the population grows. This, in turn, provides more jobs for the city's many residents.

13

Toronto's waterways have made it a popular place for trading and shipping goods. The area first became a trading post for Native Canadians when Europeans began exploring North America in the 1600s. As trade increased, more people moved to the area. It became the "Town of York" in 1793.

▼ The word "Toronto" comes from the Huron Native Canadian word for "fishing weir," as many fish were caught in Lake Ontario. This scene dates from 1842.

Yonge Street is the longest street in the world. It starts at Toronto's waterfront and travels north for 1,185 miles (1,907 km).

As the population grew, the town became the City of Toronto in 1834. Today, Toronto is still an important place for business and trade. It also remains a great place to live. Every year, new residents come to Toronto. They are drawn to the city's low crime rate, many parks, and clean streets.

Toronto families live in residential areas scattered throughout the city. For example, many schools, stores, and businesses along Bathurst Street are owned by people of the Jewish faith. Businesses and restaurants on Danford Avenue are mostly run by Greeks. Toronto's homes are a mixture of houses, townhouses, and apartments. Apartment buildings have more stories in the city center, where space is limited.

▼ Toronto's Kensington Market is a popular shopping place. Here, residents can buy fresh fish, meat, and vegetables brought in from nearby rural areas.

Some Toronto residents work or go to school near their homes. Others have to travel to other parts of the city every day. They may walk or bicycle short distances. They make longer trips by car or by bus or subway. At the end of the day, city streets become clogged with traffic as residents make their way back home.

▶ Near the center of the city, many houses are more than 70 years old. Single families used to live in them. Today, the houses are mostly divided into small apartments.

In Toronto, children go to school from September to June. In the residential areas, most children walk or bicycle to school or take a short bus ride. Clubs and sports teams are organized through school or the local community center. In the summer, the centers have many camps and outdoor pools to help stay cool.

△ Toronto students can attend public school in one of Canada's two official languages of English and French. Private schools are available in other languages.

Skaters skate by the holiday lights at Nathan Phillips Square. The rink becomes a reflecting pool in the summer.

Libraries, museums, theaters, and the Toronto Zoo are open all year long to keep people busy. On weekends, many families head downtown by subway or car. There, they can take in a show or a sporting event. They can eat at a Yonge Street restaurant or shop in the stores of Yorkville.

# Transportation

There are many ways to get around the city of Toronto. There are walkways and bike paths in each neighborhood so residents can walk or bicycle to local shops and offices. Many people use cars, but outside the residential areas, parking is expensive and hard to find. Subways or buses are good choices for getting around. They travel to most parts of the city.

▼ The Toronto Transit Commission (TTC) runs the subway system that connects city neighborhoods with one another.

Union Station is the main connecting point for many means of transportation. Here, travelers change buses, trains, or subways. They can also stay dry and warm in winter within walking tunnels that connect many downtown office buildings. Travelers can also hop on a downtown streetcar, powered by electric cables, or catch a ferry across the lake to Toronto Island.

# Local Government

Toronto's local **government** runs and organizes the city. It is located in the city center. The government is made up of councilors, who are people elected by residents from each neighborhood. The leader of the local government is the mayor. Elections are held every three to four years.

▼ Toronto is the capital of the province of Ontario. The provincial government meets in these buildings located in the city center.

Toronto's local government supplies many services for its residents. City workers keep busy collecting trash and items to **recycle**. They look after water and sewer services to make sure residents have clean water. They tend city gardens in the summer and clear snow from neighborhood streets and sidewalks in the winter. Toronto's police, fire, and medical services are all important for keeping Toronto residents safe.

23

# Through the Year

Toronto has festivals and events throughout the year. Many focus on the city's different cultures. Some, like "Taste of the Danforth," take place in residential areas. This festival is held along the Greek neighborhood's main street. Other events, such as "Caribana," are held in Toronto's city center. Caribana celebrates the Caribbean culture's music and food.

▼ Fans cheer for the Maple Leafs hockey team in the winter. In the summer, they support the Bluejays baseball team.

Summer is a busy time in Toronto. There are fireworks competitions, outdoor concerts, and dragonboat races along the city's waterfront. In the fall, city residents can catch a glimpse of their favorite movie stars at the Toronto International Film Festival. In winter, residents play hockey on indoor and outdoor rinks. Then, spring signals the start of the baseball season, garden shows, and maple syrup festivals.

▼ Toronto's climate changes with each season. Temperatures range from more than 86°F (30°C) in the summer to less than 5°F (−15°C) in the winter.

# Changing Lifestyle

Toronto's population grows each year. Many new residents come from different countries. Being a multicultural city makes Toronto a fun place to visit and live. It also takes special planning. Toronto helps its new **immigrants** by offering them services in many different languages.

▼ Trees and plants help keep the air clean. Local Toronto laws keep healthy trees from being cut down on public and private properties.

A rising population adds fresh ideas and energy to the city. It can also create challenges. Extra people produce more pollution and garbage. Toronto keeps the city clean with a city-wide program to encourage people to recycle. It has many bicycle and hiking routes and a public transit system. This encourages residents to leave their cars at home in order to help reduce pollution.

◀ Toronto's wind turbine at Exhibition Place provides enough energy for 250 homes. The city uses other types of energy, like solar power, to light bus shelters.

There are many residential cities like Toronto in the world. Each city has its own ways of managing its growing population. Cities such as Denver, Colorado, spread out in size to make room for new people. Other cities, such as Hong Kong, build tall buildings with many stories because space on the ground is limited.

▼ Delhi is the capital of India. New residents are attracted to the city because it is a central place for business and travel. It has a population of nearly 16 million.

Amsterdam in the Netherlands is a city built around canals. It has a population of about 1.4 million. Most residents travel on bicycles and trams. Cars are parked beside the canals.

As the population of Earth grows, protecting the environment becomes even more important. Urban areas with large populations affect the environment the most. Residential cities can help by enforcing rules about air, water, and ground pollution. This helps their city and surrounding areas be safer and more pleasant places to live.

### Film city
Toronto is sometimes called "Hollywood North," as many new films are shot in the city. Among the famous feature films shot here were *Transformers: Revenge of the Fallen*.

### The longest street
Yonge Street travels 1,185 miles (1,907 km) from Toronto to Rainy River, Ontario. *The Guinness Book of World Records* lists it as the longest street in the world.

### Toronto's castle
Toronto's "Casa Loma" is the only real castle in all of North America. It was built between 1911 and 1914 and cost 3.5 million dollars to build its many rooms, towers, and secret passages.

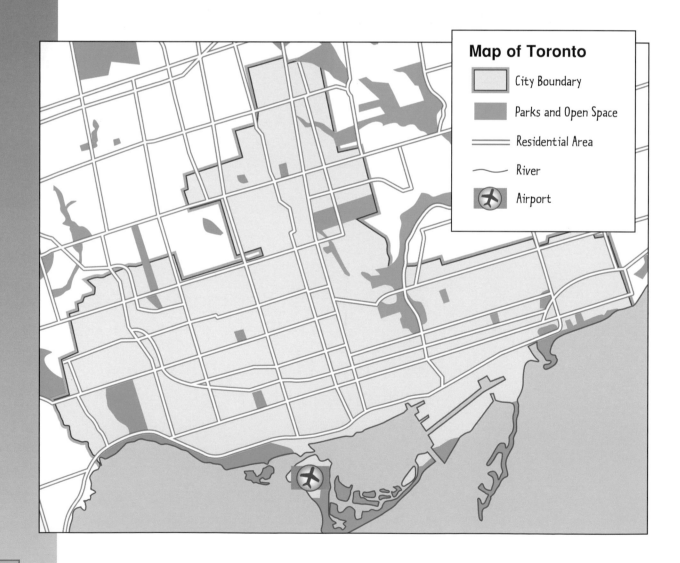

**Map of Toronto**
City Boundary
Parks and Open Space
Residential Area
River
Airport

# Glossary

**city** A large urban area, with thousands of people and many houses, offices, roads, and factories

**commercial** To do with buying and selling of goods and services

**community** A group of people who live, work, and play close together

**company** A group of people that work together to make or produce something

**construction** Repairing or making homes, buildings, or roads

**downtown** A city's central place for business, shopping, and entertainment

**energy** The power to do work. It can come from burning fuels such as coal and oil, or from wind, water, and the Sun

**factories** A business where machines are used to make something so it can then be sold

**government** People who help run communities who are usually elected by residents of the area

**immigrant** A person who comes to live in a country

**industrial** To do with industry

**multicultural** To do with the cultures of several different peoples

**natural resources** Products taken from nature like water, wood, and food

**neighborhood** A smaller community within a larger area, with its own look and customs

**population** The number of people living in an area

**recycle** To rework a product so that it can be used again

**residential** To do with local residents

**residents** People who live in a place such as a village or apartment block

**resources** Things one needs or must have

**rural** A small, quiet living area in the countryside

**suburban** A residential zone located outside the city

**town** A place where people live that has many houses, roads, and stores, and even offices and factories. Small towns can be rural, large towns are urban

**transportation** Different methods of transport

**urban** A built-up area such as a city or town

**village** A small rural area with a few houses

**warehouse** A large building to store goods

**zone** An area of a city used for a particular purpose

31

# Further Information

## FURTHER READING

*Book of Cities*, Piero Ventura, Universe Publishing, 2009.

*City Signs*, Zoran Milich, Kids Can Press, 2005.

*Toronto: City Guide.* Brian Bell, Langenscheidt Publishers, 2006.

*Toronto.* Barbara Radcliffe Rogers and Stillman D. Rogers, Children's Press, 2000.

*The Lobster Kid's Guide to Exploring Toronto.* Natalie Ann Corneau, Lobster Press, 2000.

*The Toronto Story.* Claire Mackay and Johnny Wales, Annick Press, 2002.

*What is a Community: From A to Z*, Bobbie Kalman, Crabtree Publishers, 2000.

*Wow! City!* Robert Neubecker, Hyperion Children's Books, 2004.

## WEB SITES

**Toronto Facts and Figures:** http://www.toronto.com/tiff/article/375228
**Official City of Toronto Website:** http://www.toronto.ca/index.htm
**Toronto's Hockey Hall of Fame**: http://www.hhof.com/
**CN Tower:** http://www.cntower.com/
**Toronto Maple Leafs:** http://mapleleafs.nhl.com/
**Toronto Blue Jays:** http://toronto.bluejays.mlb.com/index.jsp?c_id=tor

# Index